ART ATTACK™

HOW TO DRAW

LONDON, NEW YORK, MUNICH,
MELBOURNE and DELHI

DESIGNER Cathy Tincknell
EDITOR Cynthia O'Neill Collins
PHOTOGRAPHY Andy Crawford

BRAND MANAGER Lisa Lanzarini
PUBLISHING MANAGER Simon Beecroft
CATEGORY PUBLISHER Alex Allan
PRODUCTION Nick Seston

PROJECT MAKERS Guy Harvey, Claire Jones, Lynne
Moulding, Anne Sharples, Lisa Lanzarini,
John Kelly and Cathy Tincknell

MODELS Alfie Clarke pp 12–13 and 18–19, Harriet
Eldridge pp 46–47, Hugo Harvey pp 46–47

ADDITIONAL PHOTOGRAPHY Horse p 32 and Belgian street
scene p 38 © Dorling Kindersley Limited

Published in Great Britain in 2006 by
Dorling Kindersley Limited,
80 Strand, London WC2R 0RL

A Penguin Company

06 07 08 09 10 10 9 8 7 6 5 4 3 2 1

A CIP catalogue record for this book
is available from the British Library

ISBN-13: 978-1-40531-635-4
ISBN-10: 1-40531-635-7

Colour reproduction by Media Development and Printing Ltd, UK
Printed and bound by Toppan, Hong Kong

Doring Kindersley would like to thank Media Merchants
for their help in making this book.

www.artattack.co.uk

Discover more at
www.dk.com

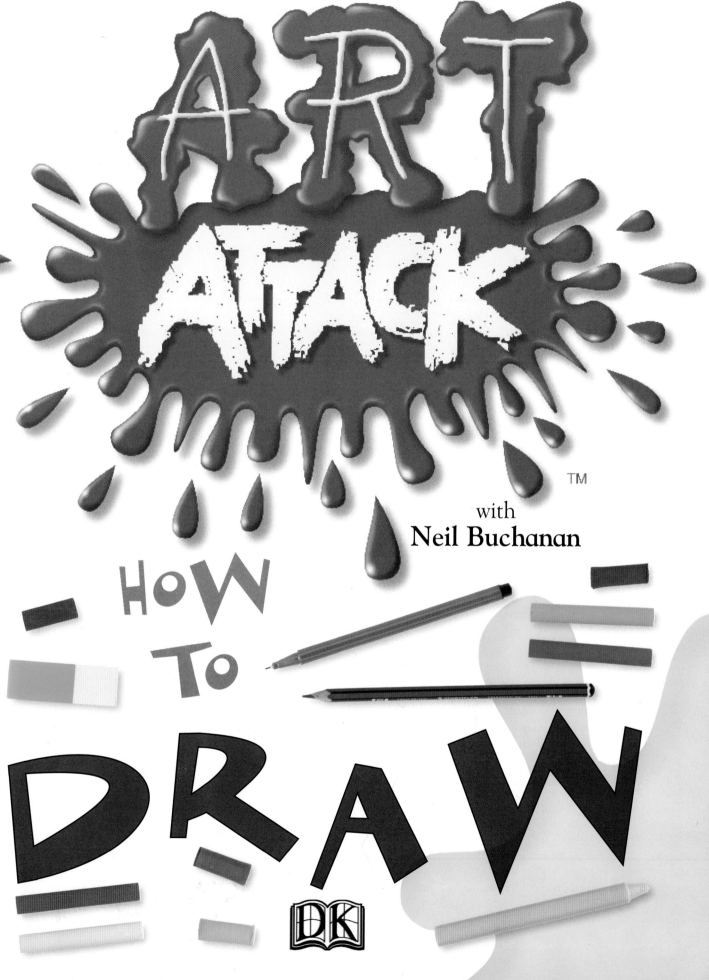

ART ATTACK

™

with
Neil Buchanan

HOW TO

DRAW

DK

Contents

Getting Started

Hello there! Do you like drawing, but don't know how to make great pictures? Then this is the book for you! It's packed with easy, fun Art Attack ideas to help you draw people and animals, places and wacky cartoons! The more you try, the easier it gets. So why not give it a go, and have an Art Attack?

Neil Buchanan

Why not try drawing with pens made from lolly sticks? See 8–9.

Scrapbook

Make a scrapbook of pictures you like, to help you collect ideas for drawing projects. Fill it with postcards, stickers and photos from old magazines. If you want to, give your scrapbook a theme: animals, interesting faces, cool buildings... You'll never be stuck for inspiration again!

Carry a sketchbook with you. When you see something interesting, draw it!

Colouring pencils

Cardboard

Oil pastels

Materials

You'll find that the more materials you try, the more effects you get. Compare how your pictures look drawn on smooth paper, or paper with a rougher surface. From white paper to cardboard boxes, have fun experimenting!

Inks

You can even paint with a washing-up sponge! See 36–37.

Chalk

Charcoal

ARTIST'S TIP

When you're trying out these Art Attacks, sketch lightly first. Then you can adjust your mistakes as you go. When you're happy with your sketch, go over it with heavier lines. People won't be able to see the wispy lines in the finished picture, because they're so light.

Equipment

What do you like to draw with? Don't just stick with your favourite drawing equipment – try lots of different kinds. Crayons, pencils, charcoal, pastels, felt-tip pens... the list goes on and on, and you'll get a different kind of picture each time.

7

You will need

Paper

Ice lolly sticks

Ink

Lolly Stick Drawing

When it comes to pen and ink pictures, you can spend a fortune on fancy pens – or you can make a masterpiece from an ordinary lolly stick!

1 Just take a lolly stick between your fingers and carefully snap off one end. You'll be left with a straight, slightly scratchy edge.

Scratchy edge

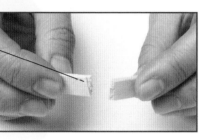

2 Hold the stick in the same way that you'd hold a pen. Dip the 'pen' into ink – and experiment!

3 Hold the end of the stick flat to the page and you'll be able to make thick, solid lines.

Remember to keep dipping the stick in the ink for solid colour

4 Twist the stick a little, so that you're just using the edge, to get thinner lines. Press firmly to make stronger lines and more gently for thin, delicate lines.

Twist to get thin lines

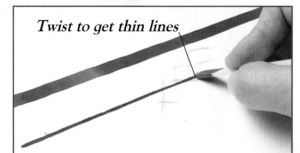

5 If you use only the pointy corner of the stick, when there's not too much ink on it, you can create fainter lines.

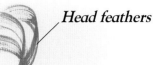

6 If you flick the stick with your finger, you get a feathered effect, like the fourth line here. And if you hold the stick in one position and draw a wavy line, you get a line that goes thick-thin-thick!

Head feathers

7 Keep experimenting, and when you're used to drawing with the stick, try a picture using all the new techniques. I've drawn a fabulous bird, but you can draw whatever you like!

Make sweeping strokes to create the flamboyant tail feathers

Make lolly pens in lots of different colours

Hold the pen flat and use short strokes for the chest feathers

Just use a little ink, and the corner of the pen, to make the short face feathers

Dab gently with the edge of the pen to make stripy rows of lines

How to Draw People

A good way to start drawing people is to think of bodies as made up of lots of simple shapes. Here's an idea for you to try.

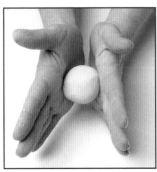

1 Begin by making three egg and eight sausage shapes from modelling clay. The sausages should be the small, thin type!

2 Lay out the sausages and eggs like a person. Make the head from one egg, the body from two more eggs, and use two sausages each to make the arms and legs.

Head

Arms

Legs

3 Try copying how the sausage-and-egg-shaped person looks.

4 Then try laying out the sausages and eggs in a different, more realistic pose, as if the person is moving. Draw the shapes in pencil as a rough outline, so you can add more detail into the picture later.

Try setting up an active pose

Rub out the pencil marks at the end

5 Turn your drawing into a picture of a person by adding hands and feet, hair and a face, as well as details like clothes and props. I've drawn a musician!

Drawing people from the side

Don't make the body any fatter than the head

You can only see one leg because it hides the other one!

3 For the arm, put a mark about halfway between the top of the legs and the knee. Don't let the finger tips go any further than that mark!

Draw in both halves of the arm, then the hand

Add a foot

1 Start with an oval head. Then draw a body about twice as long as the head.

2 The leg is about three times the length of the head. Divide it into a top half and a bottom half.

4 Use tracing paper to practise putting your sideways-on people into different shapes, and add more detail.

When you're happy with your sketches, add more details and some clothes

Add features and hair

Rub out pencil outlines

11

You will need

Pencil

Paper

Mirror

Rubber

Self-portrait

One of the best ways to teach yourself how to draw faces is to do it in front of a mirror. Let's face it – this is another great Art Attack!

1 Start by spending some time staring at yourself in a mirror. Take a good look at the shape of your face. Is it oval, round, square or long? Lightly sketch the shape of your face.

Your eyes are about halfway down your face

2 Look at the shape of your eyes. They're quite flat, a sort of oval shape, with a pointed end in the corner. Notice how your eyeballs don't go right into the corner.

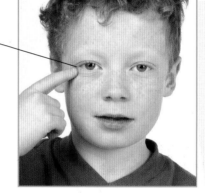

3 Draw what you see – a flattened oval with pointy ends, about halfway up your head.

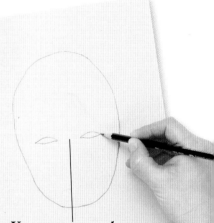

Your eyes are about an eye-width apart

The coloured part is darker around the edge

4 The coloured parts of your eyes are round, with a black circle in the middle. They're also slightly tucked under the top eyelid. Leave a highlight in the black bit.

5 Keep looking in the mirror! Look closely at the curved shapes of your eyelids and the eyebrows above them. Draw the creases of the eyelids, with curved eyebrows above.

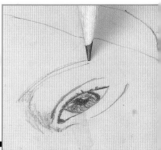

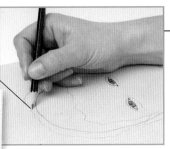

Sketch in the hair

6 Now add your nose. Draw the sides of the nostrils first, then the bobbly tip. Finish by shading the sides so your nose looks like it sticks out.

The nostrils are in shadow

7 Study your mouth, then sketch the lips lightly. Where they meet will be darker as it's in shadow. Draw what you see!

If you practise getting everything in the right position, you'll soon be drawing perfect faces

Now try drawing these!

Happy

When you're happy, your eyebrows go up and your mouth curves up at the edges

Sad

When you look sad, your eyes scrunch up and your mouth turns down

Tired

When you're tired, your whole face seems to sag, and your head seems to sink into your shoulders

Here are some more expressions. Can you guess what they are?

Paper

Pen

Let's Face It!

Here are some good tips to help you draw lots of different faces, whether you're drawing men or women, or young or old people.

Men and women

1 Remember, men tend to have larger faces and stronger ears and noses. Women tend to have daintier noses and bigger eyes.

2 Women also tend to have fuller lips. In my picture the woman has big lips, and the man a thin pair, drawn with simple lines.

3 Don't forget the neck! It's almost, but not quite, as wide as the face. From the front, it's quite straight. Men usually have thicker jaws and necks than women.

From the side, the woman's neck seems to tuck under her chin

Neck seen side-on

4 Seen from the side, a neck looks different. Here, the woman's neck slopes back slightly, and it's also slightly curved.

Neck seen from the front

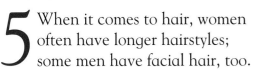

Men's eyebrows are usually a lot thicker

Women often wear more jewellery than men

5 When it comes to hair, women often have longer hairstyles; some men have facial hair, too.

Older people

1 When people are old their features look more droopy. They have droopy lips, a droopy nose and droopy eyelids!

2 They have lines on their forehead and around their face. The more lines around their face, the older you can make them look. Their chin, cheeks and neck are wrinkly and droopy, too.

Add lots of lines around the eyes

Features are droopy

3 Old men may have tufty hair on the sides of their heads. Many old ladies have curly hair.

Old ladies sometimes look a bit frail while old men look a bit more plump

Why not add a pair of spectacles?

Paper

Crayons

Pencil

Chalks or pastels

Full Speed Pictures

Do you have trouble drawing pictures with action in them? Here are a few tips to help you make your drawings look like they're really moving!

1 Decide which direction your action is going to go in, then sweep your pencil quickly across a piece of paper in the same direction.

It doesn't need to be neat!

2 Now use that guide line as the basis of a matchstick man or woman. Add his or her body, arms, legs and head, using quick, sweeping pencil lines.

Original guide line becomes side of body

3 Next, use a wax crayon to give your character a more solid shape.

Go over your pencil outlines in crayon

4 Add in some details, like a face, hair and clothes.

Speed smudging

1 Using coloured chalk, draw a ball. Looks a bit still, doesn't it? To find out how to make a ball 'move', draw just half a ball.

This technique works for anything you like – look at this puppy, racing after the ball!

2 Smudge the chalk to one side with your finger. That's enough to make the ball look like it's whizzing through the air!

5 Add props that help show what your character is doing, then colour your picture in.

This drawing of an ice dancer started as a matchstick figure too!

6 This 'matchstick man' idea works for any action picture, from football player to ice dancer. Go on, try it yourself!

Finishing Details

Here are some great tips to help you get the details just right when you're finishing off your pictures of people.

Hands

1 A lot of people find it difficult to draw hands. It's a common problem. For example, a lot of people draw hands facing forward and flat, like here. The hands just don't look quite right...

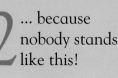

2 ... because nobody stands like this!

3 It's more like this. The boy's hands look more like claws from the front. You can't even see all of his fingers.

4 So try the 'claw' tip! Draw the thumbs on the inside, near the body. Draw the other fingers from the side, and curved. You don't need to show them all.

5 Of course, not everyone stands facing the front! If you're drawing someone sideways on, then put in all of their fingers, and make the thumb point the way the person is facing.

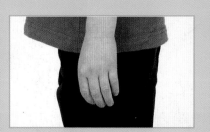

Draw a full hand with fingers for someone facing sideways

Draw a 'claw' hand for someone facing forwards

Clothes

1 Add details to clothes to stop outfits looking flat. For example, let's make this bride and groom, and the boy peeking at them, more interesting.

The fabric looks flat

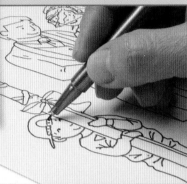

Draw lightly over the bride's face to give her a veil

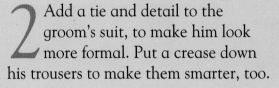

2 Add a tie and detail to the groom's suit, to make him look more formal. Put a crease down his trousers to make them smarter, too.

3 Make the boy a bit scruffier. For an untidy look, break up the lines and edges. Add some creases in his top, and in his jeans, where he's been sitting down. Don't forget his shoelaces!

Add flowing lines so the bride's dress material seems to drape

Glasses

Add the arms of the glasses. Put two lines in the opposite corners of each frame, to make them look like glass!

To draw glasses, draw the bridge of the glasses onto the bridge of the nose. Draw frames around the eyes.

The highlight makes the glasses look more realistic

For sunglasses draw frames as normal, but add a little highlight in the top corner, then colour the rest in with a dark pen.

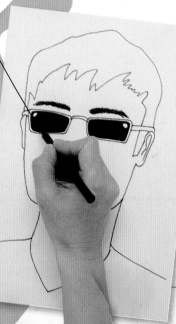

Biro 'n' Wash

Art materials are everywhere – you don't need expensive equipment! Here's a great idea for using your school pen to draw a spooky piece of art.

1 Ballpoint pens are great for sketching. Just draw with the pen as if it's a pencil. I'm drawing a picture of a witch on a moonlit flight, but you can draw whatever you like.

Press harder for strong, darker lines, or lighter for faint, wispy lines

2 Don't worry if you need to go over the pen lines to alter them. It gives the picture a scratchy feel, and that's just right for a spooky picture!

3 Shade the picture in, using the hatching technique. Just do lots of small lines, close together and all going in the same direction. You don't need to be neat....

Hatch to build up the dark areas of your picture

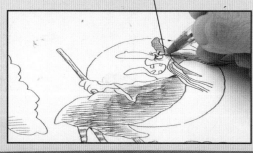

4 Then make dark areas even darker by cross-hatching. That's when you draw lines across the ones you've already done, but in the other direction.

Cross-hatching makes the clouds look fuller

Add the wash

Water the paint down a lot!

5 Now make your picture extra moody by adding soft shadows, using very watered-down paint. Brush it on, really lightly. This is called a pen and wash technique.

6 The great thing about this technique is that the ballpoint pen lines don't run when you wash over them. So you can build up lots of shades of grey with the wash.

You can even add darker shadows by adding a tiny bit more paint to the brush – but not too much

Light and Shade

Adding light and shade is guaranteed to make your pictures better, because they help make flat objects come to life.

You will need

Paper

Pencil

Chalk

Rubber

Charcoal

Arrow shows light direction

Leave the white paper showing through to create the highlight

1 This ball has light shining on it from the left. The other side is in the shade. Let's draw the ball.

2 I haven't added light and shade yet and my ball looks really flat, dull and 2-D.

3 Now I've shaded heavily on the right, darker side and kept the left lighter. My ball looks a lot more 3-D.

Light and shade make coloured pictures better, too. Darken the colours in the shady bits, and lighten them where the sun is shining on them

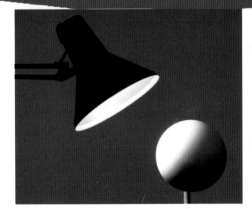

I used a rubber to create the lightest highlights

You can use a rubber to add highlights, too. Here, the light is from the window, so the side of the vase facing the window is lighter

I shaded more heavily in the areas away from the light

Chalk and charcoal

Once you've drawn all the light areas, add the shade using the charcoal, as below.

Working with chalk and charcoal can help you see the light! Start by drawing a place or person with charcoal. Next, use chalk to draw the light, or where the light is coming from.

Now that you know where the light is coming from, you can add light to the subject. Use the chalk to draw splashes of light down the edges of the figure where the light hits her.

Finally, smudge the chalk and charcoal towards each other, very lightly

Add shading on opposite edges

Chalkoal Pictures

Chalk and charcoal are great materials for drawing. Here's how to use them together to create a picture with texture, light and shade.

Begin sketching with charcoal

1 Choose something you want to draw. (If you'd like to draw a ship like me but don't know how, why not trace one from a book?) Begin by sketching the dark bits in first. Use charcoal, and draw your picture on coloured paper.

2 When you use charcoal, you don't have to be neat or perfect, because if you make a mistake, you can just rub it out with your finger!

Charcoal rubs away easily

Use light, quick strokes with the chalk to add highlights to your ship

3 Decide where the light is coming from. Once you've done that, you can draw the chalk along the edges that are facing the light, to make highlights. Here, the moonlight is shining onto the left-hand side of the ship's sails and masts.

Add chalk highlights

Try different types of line

4 Use the charcoal for the shady bits – that is, the bits away from the light, like the sails themselves.

5 The great thing about charcoal is that you can create an atmospheric shadowy effect by lightly smudging it. Gently smudge the sails with your finger, to make shadows. And there it is, a chalkoal picture. Try it yourself!

Add some waves and moonlight

You will need

Pencil   Paper

Colouring pencils

Animal Shapes

Animals might seem hard to draw but, if you break them down into simple shapes, you can create great pictures. Here are some ideas.

1 Draw a dog. Use a pencil to draw a round circle for the head, a long, slightly pointed oval for the snout, and then the numbers 6, 1, 1, 1. Keep the three 1s close together.

2 Use this as a guide to drawing your dog. First put in his features – his eyes, the shape of his snout and ears, and the rest of his head.

3 Add fur to the body shape along the 6, draw in a tail, and then use the 1s as your guide shape to draw the legs and paws. Draw in a collar around your dog's neck.

The 6 is the guide shape for your dog's body

Keep numbers close to make a thinner dog

Spread the numbers out to draw a stocky dog

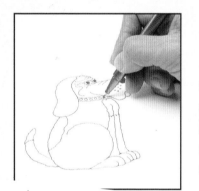

4 Use this tip as the basis for any dog you like. Why not try making the numbers 6 and 1 different sizes, and moving them together or apart? See how it changes the kind of dog you get!

Floppy ears

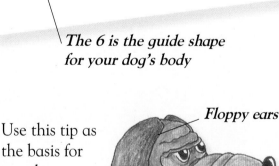

1 This shark was drawn from triangles! Start with a big triangle for the body, a medium-sized one for the head, and lots of small ones for the fins.

Make the mouth and teeth from triangles, too

Draw lightly in pencil and rub out the guide triangles once you've finished

2 Round the triangles off and add slightly curved lines for gills, to complete a great drawing of a shark.

Put the eyes at the top of the face

Shark turning

Round the triangles off once you've finished

Shark, seen from below

3 The technique works for different views of a shark. Here's a drawing of a shark coming at you!

4 You can draw any view of a shark using triangles. Just round off the shapes to complete your picture.

Beady eyes

Pricked-up ears

Fluffy coat

Plain collar

Spots

Fancy poodle clipping

Shaggy fur

Novelty collar

27

Easy Dinosaurs

Here are some great tips to help you draw dinosaurs, using simple shapes to start, and then adding lots of texture and detail.

1 Begin by drawing an oval for the body. Then add a curved neck and tail. These should be chunky near the body, then thinner towards the tip.

2 If you run out of space for the tail, turn it back on itself. Draw legs that look a bit like fat sausages, curving outwards.

3 The head, in comparison to the neck, is quite tiny, with a long snout.

Thick, muscular neck

Draw the shapes in pencil first

4 Next, draw another dinosaur, this time starting with a big, diamond-shaped body. Draw a slightly smaller diamond for the head, and for the big back legs draw a mini diamond shape, pointing down.

5 Add a tail and two little claw-like arms. Add the back legs by drawing lines backwards, then forwards.

Finish by adding feet

Colouring pencils (or you could use crayons)

6 Give both your dinosaurs a face (if you like, add a mouth full of huge teeth!). Then, using a dark green pencil, go round the outlines to break the shapes up. Make the dinosaurs lumpy, especially around the legs.

Add curved wrinkles to the dinosaur's legs

7 Draw long grooves down the dinosaurs' backs and up their necks, and one down their stomachs and tails. This makes them look more muscular. Wrinkly grooves down the legs make them look old, but sturdy.

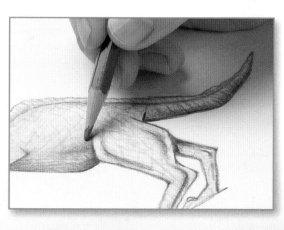

8 Build up wrinkles and muscles all over the dinosaurs' bodies.

Add highlights in white

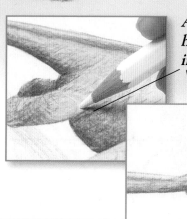

9 When you're colouring the dinosaurs in, don't just use dark green. Try some lighter green bits, and a hint of yellow all over for a reptilian feel. Add white highlights around the legs, and some darker shading on their stomachs to make your dinosaurs look 3-D!

Fluff 'n' Stuff

Do you want to make your animal drawings look soft and fluffy? If you'd like to know how to draw cuter animals, then read on!

1 Start by sketching a kitten. Just think of it as lots of soft, round shapes. Draw a circle for the head, and two larger ovals for the body, all quite close together.

Head

Body

Draw the paws as ovals, too

2 Draw four smaller ovals for the big paws, not too far from the body as kittens have short legs.

Draw round the ovals to link them up

3 Next, draw around the body and head shapes, to connect them up. Sketch in the legs and add a little pointy tale.

Add a nose

4 Now give your kitten a face. Start with a tiny, triangular nose in the middle of its head.

5 Add two dots for the eyes, a smile and a set of whiskers. Don't forget to put in the ears too!

The whiskers should be beneath your kitten's nose

6 But this kittten doesn't look fluffy – yet. That's because its outline has been drawn with a thick, unbroken pencil line.

7 Use a pen to give the kitten a dotty outline instead.

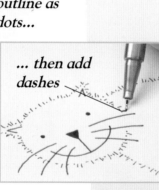

Start the outline as dots...

A good tip to remember is that the less dashes you put in, the softer the fur looks

8 Then add some dashes between the dots. Can you see what happens? A soft, fluffy kitten emerges.

... then add dashes

9 You can do the same thing for chicks or bunnies too – just base your drawing on soft, rounded shapes.

Draw a Horse

If you've ever had problems drawing horses, now is the time to cheat! Just use the 'simple shapes' guidelines to make it a lot easier.

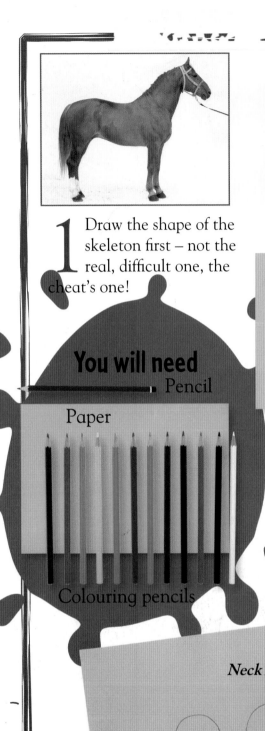

1 Draw the shape of the skeleton first – not the real, difficult one, the cheat's one!

You will need

Pencil

Paper

Colouring pencils

2 Start with two circles, one a bit bigger than the other. That's the front of your horse. Keep a gap between the circles.

Knees

3 Next, draw in lines for the front legs. Make the back legs slightly angled back. Add two small circles halfway down each leg for the knees, and two small circles at the ends for the ankles.

4 Now draw in a line for the neck, and two circles for the head, one slightly bigger than the other. That completes the cheat's skeleton!

Neck   *Head*

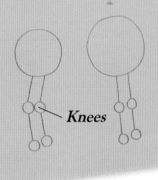

Keep the line softly curved

5 Use the lines as a guide to putting in the shape of the horse. Start by joining the big circles with curved lines.

6 Using light strokes, fatten out the legs, making them thicker at the top. Thicken up the neck and draw in the shape of the head.

Horses have strong, thick necks

Add the ears

7 Add in pointy, triangular ears, a mane and a tail. Add hooves, which look a bit like triangles, to the front of the ankles.

Add the hooves to the front of the ankles

Draw in a thick mane

8 Finally, don't forget the nostril, mouth and eye. That completes the basic horse shape. Now you can use the skeleton to make the picture more 3-D.

Dark eyes

Large nostril

Tail stretches almost to the top of the knees

9 When you colour in your horse, shade more around the bottom edges of all of the circles, to give the impression of roundness and muscles. Shade in along the other skeleton guidelines, and the horse's muscle structure will start to appear.

You can rub out pencil guides when you're finished

Make sure that the far legs are coloured a bit darker, so that they look further away than the near legs

You will need

Paper

Pencil

Oil pastels or wax crayons

Cheat's Landscape

Do you find drawing a country scene hard? Here's an easy way to do it – but don't tell anyone you've been cheating!

Wavy lines

1 Draw a wavy line about three-quarters of the way up the paper. Draw three more lines underneath. Make the lines further apart as you go down the page.

Link the lines up

2 Next, make some of the wavy lines join up with the wavy lines underneath them.

Join up some of the lines in the foreground in the same way

3 Look – you've drawn some rolling hills! Now add bushes and trees. The further away they are, the smaller and less detailed they need to be.

Make the trees and hedges different shapes and sizes

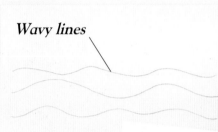

4 Add some parallel lines, to make fields for crops to grow in.

5 Add farm buildings too. Put them in the middle of the picture.

Draw lines to suggest windows and doors

Country roads can be quite bendy!

6 Add a road, snaking over the hills toward the farms. Just draw two lines that go in the same direction. You can even add a little stream – make sure you add some small squiggles so it looks like water!

Oil Pastels

Try rich, green oil pastels to colour your landscape. They will blend beautifully.

Blending with circular motion

Blending with sideways motion

7 Once you've drawn out the landscape, colour it in. Remember, the further away the fields are, the lighter shade of green they should be.

Add soft, fluffy clouds

You will need

Paper

Pastels

Poster paint

Old washing-up sponge

Country Tips

Here are ideas to help you get your country pictures full of realistic detail, from rolling hills to the leaves on the trees!

1 Draw the sun into your picture. The position of the sun shows you where to put shadows later.

Put the sun to the right or left of the page, but not in the middle

2 Draw a few hill shapes, and then draw a long, slightly flattened, letter C down the middle of each hill.

Use a green pastel to draw the hills

C shape

Shadows on the side away from the sun

Sunlight makes this side of the hill lighter

3 Colour the side of the hill nearer to the sun with a light green. Colour the other side with a darker green. You will start to get the effect of rolling hills, with shadows on one side.

MOUNTAINS

This tip works for mountains too! Colour one side of the mountain lightly, and make the other side slightly darker – it makes the mountains look more 3-D.

4 In the front of your picture draw a tree trunk, with branches but no leaves. Remember, branches don't all grow from the trunk – some grow and fork out from other branches.

Branches get thinner, the further they are from the tree trunk

Colour in the foreground, too

5 Now add leaves – the easy way! Dip a piece of washing-up sponge into green poster paint that's been thinly spread on a saucer.

Add darker green for shady bits

Add yellow around the top edge of the tree where the light is catching it

6 Now print it onto your picture. The sponge will print textured 'leaves' onto your tree.

You can use this technique for grass, too!

7 For a drawing on blue paper, pastels are good for clouds. Just draw an irregularly-shaped cloud.

Build up the edges with the chalk on its side

8 Finally, add some touches of sunlight on the edge of the hills to bring them to life.

If you like, add more detail in the foreground with chalks

In the Distance

You will need

Rubber
Pencil
Ruler
Paper
Colouring pencils

Your pictures will look more realistic if objects seem smaller, the more distant they are. This is called perspective.

Vanishing point

Horizon

Look at this photo of a street. Now look at it again, with the guidelines printed on top. The place where the lines seem to

meet and disappear is called the vanishing point. Artists use vanishing points to help them create distance in pictures.

Horizon

Vanishing point

1 Draw a street, using a vanishing point. Begin by deciding where the horizon will be. Mark the vanishing point on it.

2 Now roughly sketch in the side of a house, including the side of the roof, in the spot where you want it to be. Add a tree opposite the house.

Guides run from the vanishing point to the edge of the house

Vanishing point

Vanishing point

Guidelines

3 Using a ruler lightly draw guidelines from the vanishing point to the edges of the house and tree.

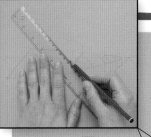

The edges of the roofs are parallel to each other, and kept within the guides

4 Draw more trees and houses, keeping them within the guide lines. Add doors and windows to your houses. Remember, all these details must get smaller and closer together as they go into the distance.

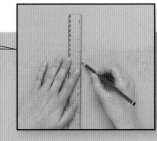

The vertical lines are parallel, too

5 When you've added the finishing details, colour your picture in. Rub out the guidelines that you used and show off your masterpiece!

The road gets thinner

Things look more faded in the distance

Use stronger colours in the foreground (front) of your picture

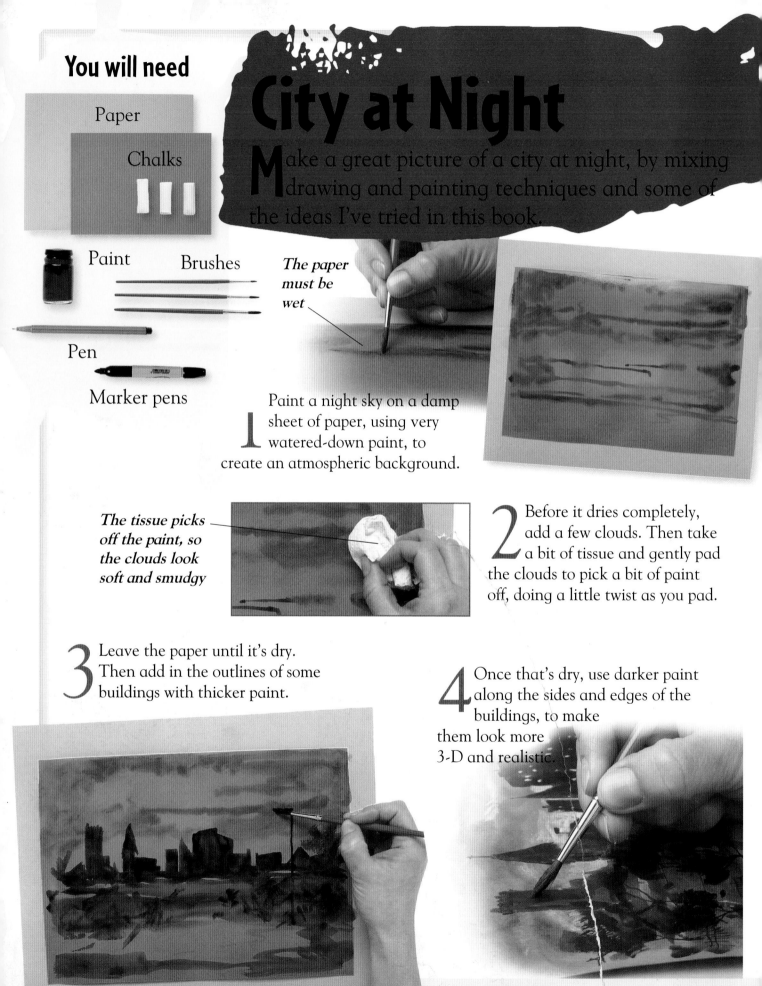

You will need

Paper

Chalks

Paint   Brushes

Pen

Marker pens

City at Night

Make a great picture of a city at night, by mixing drawing and painting techniques and some of the ideas I've tried in this book.

The paper must be wet

1 Paint a night sky on a damp sheet of paper, using very watered-down paint, to create an atmospheric background.

The tissue picks off the paint, so the clouds look soft and smudgy

2 Before it dries completely, add a few clouds. Then take a bit of tissue and gently pad the clouds to pick a bit of paint off, doing a little twist as you pad.

3 Leave the paper until it's dry. Then add in the outlines of some buildings with thicker paint.

4 Once that's dry, use darker paint along the sides and edges of the buildings, to make them look more 3-D and realistic.

5 When that's dry, draw in more detail with pens. Use a thin pen to add birds, streetlamps, or grass. Give trees some wispy branches.

The marker will easily cover the thin paint underneath

6 Add in a car in the foreground with a thicker marker pen.

Use chalk for lit windows in buildings

7 Finally, use chalks to give the effect of car headlamps and streetlights, and bring your picture to life!

Pen

Paper and
tracing paper

Pencil

Colouring pens

Cartoon Characters

Have you ever wanted to create your own cartoon character? Then why not start now, with this great Art Attack?

1 Take a piece of paper, and experiment with drawing facial features, starting with the eyes. There are lots of different types and they can show lots of different moods, from startled to just plain tired!

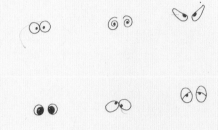

Try out different nose shapes

Experiment with mouth shapes

2 Try out different noses, too. What about a button nose, or a big round nose, or a long pointy nose, or a turned-up nose? Or two little nostrils, or maybe a warty nose...?!

3 And what about mouths? A tiny mouth, a wobbly mouth, an evil mouth, a cheesy smiley mouth, a wide mouth, a goofy mouth....

4 You don't have to do these styles, though. Do anything you like, and then mix and match them up. And that's where tracing paper comes in. Using the tracing paper, select the eyes, nose and mouth you like best.

Using the tracing paper you can create loads of different possibilities!

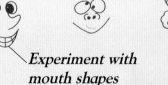

5 Use the tracing paper to make a mix-and-match face (I chose the round eyes and nose, and the goofy teeth). Then add on a body to create your cartoon character.

Experiment with colour

ARTIST'S TIP

Lots of cartoonists have their own style, and a recognisable gimmick. Their characters might have big noses, or oddly-shaped heads. So why not try it yourself – pick one strange feature, and try to draw lots of characters using that gimmick.

Characters all have beady eyes

6 When you've got your character, try giving him different outfits – it can really change his personality!

You can make a cartoon family by using the same features, but changing them a bit each time

Pen

Paper

Colouring pens

Cartoon World

Now that you know how to create your own cartoon character, learn how to draw cartoon worlds too, full of fun objects and atmosphere!

1 You can give any inanimate object a fun cartoon personality! We're starting with a balloon and an old pot of paint.

Grumpy balloon

Paint looks like hair

2 To bring them to life, just add characteristics and features, like faces or limbs.

3 You can even use specific parts of the object as props for the new character. The handle of my paint tin has become a pair of headphones! Once you've brought the objects to life, colour them in.

Now our cartoon objects are going to appear in a noisy cartoon world, with sound effects! These are an easy way to add fun to your cartoons. You just spell the sound out, then put other effects around the word. Look at the examples on the next page...

AAARGHH !!

4 To draw someone screaming, spell out the scream as it comes from their mouth. The longer you make it, the bigger the scream. It really comes to life if you add a jagged box around the scream.

The little girl screams when the bully tries to take her balloon

BANG

5 To draw the sound 'bang', such as here when the bully pops the balloon, you can put a spiky box around the word to show how startling and loud it is.

HA, HA!

SPLOSH

When the bully puts his foot in the paint, he makes a wet, 'splosh' sound

SLOP SLOP

TRIP

6 Sound effects help you to tell the story when you draw a cartoon strip. Can you work out how what happens to the bully from these final pictures? Why not experiment with drawing sounds yourself?

Half-and-half Caricatures

A caricature is a drawing that exaggerates a person's features to make them look funny or outrageous. Here's a great idea to try!

You will need

Paper

Pencil

Pen

Old photos

Colouring pencils

Keep this as reference

1 Find an old photo of a friend, and cut it in half. Move the bottom half to one side.

2 Replace the bottom half of the photo with a drawing of the person's face – but exaggerate their distinctive features!

3 Pay attention to their chin and mouth. Exaggerating these can really change the shape of a person's face.

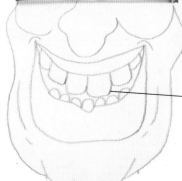

This girl now has an extra-wide, cheesy smile!

Why not really exaggerate their teeth and lips?

Try to match the colours from the original photo

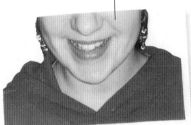

4 When you've finished, colour it in. Try to match the colours closely to the original picture.

It's easier to match the exact shade with colouring pencils

Carefully draw around the edge

5 Draw a black felt pen line around the photo and drawing when you've finished, to bring it all together – and there you have it!

Impress your friends with your new skills!

Side-by-side picture

VARIATIONS

Why not draw a caricature of the top half of your friend's face instead? Or cut the photo in half lengthways, for a side-by-side caricature!

Caricature the top half of the face

Glossary

Blend
To mix colours into each other, little by little, so that they seem to join up

Caricature
A drawing that exaggerates a person's appearance or main features to make them look funny or outrageous

Cartoon
A fun drawing of a person or thing

Charcoal
A drawing tool made from charred wood that makes soft, dark lines which smudge well

Hatching and cross-hatching
Hatching is drawing lines close together to add shade to a picture. Cross-hatching is similar, but involves drawing lines across each other

Highlight
The bright part of a drawing

Horizon
The line where the earth and the sky seem to meet

Pastels and chalks
Drawing tools. Chalk pastels are soft and oil pastels are stickier. Both kinds are really good for blending different colours together

Perspective
The way distance makes an object look smaller and further away

Portrait
Picture of a person's face

Proportions
The size of one thing compared to another

Shading
Making part of your drawing darker, to help your picture look more 3-D

Texture
The surface of, or the impression of surface in, a drawing

Vanishing point
A point on the horizon of a picture where parallel lines seem to meet

Wash
When very watered down ink or paint is used to fill in large areas of a picture